IF I KNEW THEN WHAT I KNOW NOW

"The BEST Is Yet To COME"

Jennifer Webb Farris

authorHOUSE®

AuthorHouse™
1663 Liberty Drive
Bloomington, IN 47403
www.authorhouse.com
Phone: 1 (800) 839-8640

*Scripture quotations marked KJV are from the Holy
Bible, King James Version (Authorized Version). First
published in 1611. Quoted from the KJV Classic Reference
Bible, Copyright © 1983 by The Zondervan Corporation.*

Published by AuthorHouse 09/19/2017

ISBN: 978-1-5246-9709-9 (sc)
ISBN: 978-1-5246-9708-2 (e)

Library of Congress Control Number: 2017909399

Print information available on the last page.

*Any people depicted in stock imagery provided
by Thinkstock are models, and such images are
being used for illustrative purposes only.
Certain stock imagery © Thinkstock.*

This book is printed on acid-free paper.

I dedicate this book to my family:

Your encouragement has inspired me to
be All that God has called me to be.

To my mother, Ossie Webb, the anointing
in your life and your acceptance
and support in All things has made
the difference in my life.

To my husband, Darin Farris
You inspire me more than you may ever
know. I thoroughly enjoy being your wife.

INTRODUCTION

Have you ever had an experience in which you wish you could have a do over? The purpose of this book is to help with making better decisions. Even if you are in the place where you want to be and everything is going the way you want it to go, it is possible to make better decisions.

By reading this book and applying the thoughts and ideal you will be able to effectively think things through and eventually find more joy and peace in your life.

CONTENTS

CHAPTER ONE

THE THINGS I SAY

(That Ruin My Day)

Chaotic or stressful situations may cause us say things that, without them, we may not say.

I was sitting in the very cluttered living room of the home of an acquaintance when, suddenly, her children came running in. They were loud and fast; running from one room to another. They ran as though they had a perfect game of follow the leader going on. One after the other they ran and shouted. They were disheveled but zealous.

This was my first time in her home. As I sat there, I began to wonder. Does their mother really let them run through the house like this?

Why doesn't she say something to them? Should I say something?

Minute after minute these children ran and screamed until finally one of the children came over to me and ask me; "why are you in my house?" He said it with such authority and confidence. I responded to him, "I'm waiting on your mother." He suddenly began screaming, "Momma, momma, Momma there is a lady out here." When he did not hear a response from his mother he began yelling again. I tried to let him know that she knew I was there and it was okay, but he did not listen to me. He just continued to yell until his mother responded to him by yelling from the back room.

After all the yelling, I got the attention of one of the other children and asked, don't yall want to go back outside? He responded; "No, it's hot out there."

Finally I found myself saying:

> ***"Oh my god, these children are running me crazy..."***

In the office, the phone begins to ring; one call after the other. As soon as I begin working on one project, my supervisor gives me another. She tells me, I need this yesterday. I know you may be working on something else, but I need you to have this to me before the end of the day. Not only should there be a few days devoted to this project, now it requires cleaning up what someone else messed-up.

All of a sudden, here comes the words:

> **This makes me sick, I'm tired of having to clean up someone else's mess. It pisses me off that people don't do their job.**

Many times in the workplace, it is likely to have duties transposed. Many times this happens suddenly and without notice, which could cause chaos. This chaos could lead us to say things that seem like they are innocent and have no lasting impression, but how true is that? Simple words like:

> **I'm tired of this...**

If we are not careful; we could allow these things to frustrate us. Frustrations could cause us to say even more things like:

> **I am so overwhelmed or I am so frustrated right now.**

It may seem that these are just simple words that do not matter, but it is easy to forget and some do not believe it, but **words have power**. Frustrations cause us to say things like:

> **I'm about to lose my mind.**

We all understand that chaos or troubling situations do not feel good. No one goes out looking to find chaos. Some may actually look for trouble because he or she thinks the risk will be exciting. However, no one wants to deal with problems. The bottom line is, we all have to deal with them; sometimes on a daily basis. Some of us have more chaos than others. Could it be that we cause more problems to come onto ourselves by saying negative things?

It is possible that the words we speak will affect our daily activities. After a stressful day at work, we get into our car where, we can finally put the day behind us, but not just yet; now there is the traffic to deal with. Just one more thing adding to an already stressful day.

The car could be a place of relief to help us overcome the frustrations of the workplace and get in a better place before getting home to our family. Unfortunately, because we have spoken so many negative words over, it becomes difficult to overcome these frustration and the simple issues of traffic could add to the frustrating fire already burning in our minds.

Think about it, you're ready to put an end to the frustrating day and your 20 minute commute has suddenly turned into 45 because traffic has come to a slow crawl or maybe even a screeching halt. Next thing you know, here comes more of those words:

This is a day from Hell.

Saying things like this, focuses on the negativity. It magnifies the frustrations. We have the opportunity to change the course.

At any point, we could chose to say something positive which could offset the negative.

Regardless of the situation, we should always try to find the positive. Romans 8:28 says, **"All things work together for good..."** Therefore, no matter what the situation is, there is good in it. Sometimes we just have to work at finding it, but the good is there; somewhere. Does good somehow become less good because we have to look for it?

No matter what the day delivers, if we remember Psalms 118:24 (KJV) **"this is a day that the Lord has made I will rejoice and be glad in it."** These words allow us to focus on the positive. If we focus on the positive, the negative will not be as effective. The thing that we focus on, is the thing that grows because the attention is feeding the situation.

Every day we deal with people and situations that we cannot control. Some of us seem to deal with difficult people and situations more than others but we have to remember, we have a choice. Deuteronomy 30:19 says chose life...

The power of the tongue is massive. Therefore, we must put as much effort as we need into finding positive words to counter the negative.

It's amazing how often negative words make their way through our day.

Things like:

**I'm never gonna get this, I hate my...,
I am so stupid, I cannot believe
I just did that, My crazy self, My
dumb self, I should have known I
couldn't make it, Nobody likes me,
Nobody understands me, People don't
want to spend time with me, I will
never be happy, I will never make
it to the top, I don't have any
friends, My children are bad, Why
don't my children act like..., Why are
my children so bad, I always have
to struggle, I come from the wrong
family, I come from the wrong side
of the tracks, I'm not pretty enough,
I'm too fat, I'm too skinny, I hate
my body**

These are common phrases that we say without realizing the impact. As a matter of fact, we would not appreciate anyone saying any of these words to us, so why would we say them to ourselves.

If we are going to speak such damnation upon ourselves, we do not need enemies.

Think about it, when we look at a newborn we do not tell it what it cannot do. Looking a baby we tell him or her all kinds of things that, as a baby, is impossible for them to do.

We look at babies and call them doctors, lawyers, astronauts, teachers, ball players, preachers, and many other positive and successful professionals. Looking at these small creatures we speak positively over them. Even if their parents are addicts or any other degenerates who are not doing anything positive with their life, we never look at a child and call them a loser, liar, dummy, stupid, or anything else derogatory.

So where does negativity come from?

Why is it so easy to speak negative as opposed to positive?

Over the years, as we grow older we begin to lean to our own understanding of things. Derogatory thoughts are learned. As we grow older, we learn logic. Logic tells us to deal with the situation. Dealing with the situations requires us to focus on the situation. By focusing on the situation and applying logic to it, we rule out faith.

Logic overwhelms faith causing us to doubt. Doubt then begins to take place in our words. For some reason, instead of encouraging ourselves, we are more likely to make derogatory comments. These derogatory comments cause us to miss out on the blessed places of God.

Logic tells us that conditions, medical and mental, can be hereditary. Logic says it is inevitable that it is most likely that we will contract the condition.

Faith says, all things are possible to those who believe. According to Romans 12:2 we are to be transformed by the renewing of our minds.

Through our belief and the words of our mouths we do not have to be bound by bloodlines or anything else.

We all have the ability, through our words, to speak life. By being positive in our words we can begin to think positive. Thinking positive will help us make healthy decisions. Making healthy decisions can help us to be healthy. Sure problems will still come. Struggles will even occur. However, we do not have to allow the problem to dictate to us. We may not always be able to control the situation but we can control our reactions. No matter what is going on, find a way to speak positive. Remember, your words are life or death, so I encourage you to rejoice. **No matter what; rejoice.**

This may take some practice, but practice makes perfect.

CHAPTER TWO

BE THE DIFFERENCE

(You Can Make a Change)

Regardless of where you are in life or no matter what your affairs are currently, one thing is true for each of us; if it has not already happened to you, something will come along, that will shake in a way, that will cause you to think or maybe even utter the words;

> *"I never would have thought this would happen to me." Or "I never would have thought I would find myself in this place".*

Whether the situation or place you are unexpectedly finding yourself in is a good place or a bad place, unexpectedness has the potential to cause us to make some poor decisions. It is

11

important to understand that making decisions is something that cannot be avoided in our day to day activities. We make decisions many times throughout the day. The decisions we make may directly affect us or they may indirectly affect us through the lives of a loved one or an associate.

The decisions we make could be considered good or poor. Many times, one could determine a good or poor decision by how much thought has been put into making the decision. However, there are times that even with much thought we could still make a poor decision. For example, I remember making a decision to change jobs. The company I was being offered a position with was one I had tried several times to join, with no success. Now, they were calling me. I made the decision and left the company I was currently working with. I was offered much more money and benefits, which I currently did not have. However, the time with the company was short lived.

This was a good decision, however after only a short while with the company, the doors were closed forever, as the result of someone else's poor decisions.

Yes, it is true; unfortunately, even good experiences or situations have the potential to cause us to make poor decisions. Good experiences could also cause us to end up in a bad place. Something does not have to be the worst thing for us to do the wrong thing.

Think about it; do you know anyone who went from nothing to abundance and right back to nothing. Going from nothing to abundance is a good thing. However, without guidance and direction, it is possible for a person with this newly gained abundance to make decisions that could cause them to lose everything they gained and maybe even end up worse than they were before coming into the abundance.

This maybe in the form of purchases that could bring harm or even detriment to themselves or others. This is often seen in celebrities.

Of course not all celebrities make poor decisions. However, many times when someone is raised or lives in impoverished situations and is suddenly thrust into the limelight or comes into large amounts of money, it is likely that they will begin to purchase and pursue things that are not necessarily healthy or good for them.

One example of this is professional athletes. Many times, professional athletes come from poor upbringings. However their skills far exceed expectations, which could allow them to suddenly be thrusted into the limelight. When this happens, these athletes could suddenly be given millions of dollars and with little to no direction.

When this happens, these athletes may purchase items they were never able to afford before. Who wouldn't, right? If you wanted something and was never able to obtain it because of money, wouldn't that be one of the first things you seek after coming into more than enough money to purchase that item and much more?

The unfortunate thing with this mindset is, it allows one to develop a collage of poor decisions. Poor decisions have a way having lasting effects. One poor decision could cause one to lose their newly gained abundance just as quickly as it came into his or her life. Losing these monies could ultimately cause one to lose those items he or she has purchased.

Imagine this; a purchase of a vehicle in excess of $100,000 would yield insurance and tax payments that may exceed what some people make in a year. With this in mind, if the millions, which were used to make the purchase, were suddenly gone, how could one continue to make the necessary insurance and tax payments as well as any maintenance? Without the millions, it is likely that these expensive possessions could soon be gone.

Making wiser decisions could help one obtain and maintain possessions.

When persons who may have never balanced a checkbook are suddenly thrust into the limelight or suddenly have the responsibility of managing thousands or maybe even millions of dollars, guidance and direction are needed to do so properly. There is absolutely nothing wrong with suddenly coming into abundance. As a matter of fact, Deuteronomy 28:2 (KJV) says "blessings shall overtake you." When something is overtaken it is likely that whatever was over taken was caught off guard. Who wouldn't want to be caught off guard by a blessing?

"Troubles catch us off guard, so why not a Blessing"

When our lives are pleasing to God, we should expect abundant blessings. The blessings of the Lord make rich and add no sorrow (Proverbs 10:22 KJV). Therefore, if we are putting true thought into our decisions it is likely that they will be good for us.

All decisions have rippling effects. However the ripples from poor decisions could cause so much damage that the ripples from poor decisions could have the tendency to have more lasting effects than those of good decision. Some ripples from poor decisions could cause one to get involved in illegal activities which could cause them to end up behind bars. Many times poor decisions are made quickly and without much thought.

Anyone can randomly and reactively make poor decisions. However, each of us must put forth the effort to ensure we think before we act.

One thing to keep in mind is; is the situation going to control you or are you going to take control of the situation. Taking control of a situation does not mean that the situation is under control. It simply means that although may be in a struggle, we can remain in peace. Isaiah 26:3 KJV says "he will keep us in **perfect peace**..." We have a choice and a decision to make in these difficult times.

We could choose to focus on the situation, but why. Keeping our mind on the positive is so much more rewarding. Yes, even in bad situations, there is a positive. Sometimes we have to look for it. We may even have to **diligently** look for it, but it is there. If we trust God, regardless of the situation we find ourselves in, we will not be ashamed by the decisions we make and the decision we make will work for our good.

Anyone can get upset when things do not go as planned or when something bad happens to them, but not everyone can make a difference. It's not easy to keep a positive outlook on life when bad things happen, but it is possible. It's not easy to remember that the sun will shine again when storm winds are raging, but we can be the difference. It's not easy to smile when we are in the midst of losing things we hold dear, but we can be the difference. It's easy to keep the faith, when the situation is telling us that we are being targeted, but we can be the difference.

Most people believe that when something bad happens to them, they are entitled to feel bad and behave inappropriately. They are not willing to deny themselves or their feelings. Ephesians 4:26 KJV says, be angry and sin not… This lets us know that there is nothing wrong with being upset when things do not go the way we expected them to go. However, just because we get upset or angry, does not mean that we have to lose it. If we work at it, we will realize that the sun will shine again, the storm winds will not blow forever, the struggle will not last, we can be the difference.

When making a difference, sometimes it may seem as though things we are being treated unfairly. When making a difference, sometimes we may have to apologize for something we did not do. Making a difference is not comfortable. Making a difference is not popular. Sometimes when making a difference, we may have to stand alone. Making a difference requires us to put forth a special effort. Making a difference may go against logic. Therefore, we must put forth special effort to go against what seems like the logical thing to do.

There are times when making a difference that we may go against what others have told us to or not to do.

Sometimes we may be in difficult or stormy situations as a result of poor decisions we made. Other times the difficult situation may be the result of something that was done to use by someone else. No matter how or why the difficult situation is in our life, the bottom line is, we can make a difference.

Consider the story of Job in the bible. Job was perfect and stayed away from the very appearance of evil. However, in one day, he lost everything. The story of Job allows us to see just how easily it is to be put in an extreme or difficult situation. Job had not done anything to merit him losing all that he had worked diligently to obtain. He lost his health, possessions, money, the ability to make money and yes, in this very same day, Job lost all of his children. A parent should never have to bury a child, yet Job had to bury all of his children, at one time. However, with all of what he lost, Job never lost his faith. He did not question why any of this was happening to him. He stood firm on believing that God is still worthy of praise.

By examining the story of Job, we are able to see the difference one person can make.

In the face of adversity, Job gave God praise. While standing alone, Job gave God praise.

Job stood and made a difference against those closest to him. He stood against the advice of his closest friends and his wife. Job's wife told him, "Curse God and Die" (Job 2:9 KJV). His friends accused him of sinning (Job 4 KJV). Job could have followed the advice of his wife. He could have taken the counsel of his friends. Instead he held to his integrity and continued to trust God.

Having the support of someone who knows and loves you when going through difficult situations could make a huge difference in our success with the situation.

Maybe Job's wife couldn't deal with losing everything. Maybe she couldn't deal with seeing the man she loved suddenly become morbidly ill. Maybe she thought what was happening was not fair. She knew her husband was a man of integrity. She knew it was not likely that he had done anything wrong, yet he was still suffering.

How do you think you would feel if you lived a life of integrity and suddenly you were in the midst of losing everything you worked diligently to obtain, and the people who know you better than anyone began accusing you instead of supporting and encouraging you?

I have heard it said, "you don't have to run down a lie." My dad would say, "the truth will come out in the house wash." Although Job was being accused, he did not try to prove the accusation wrong. He simply let them accuse him. He could have gotten angry or felt sorry for himself, but he did not. He continued to trust God.

Making a difference does not mean that we have to prove ourselves. Making a difference does not mean we have to try to convince others of our good or faithfulness.

When we encourage others and lift them up, we are making a difference. When we make a difference, we realize that we do not have to be the one in the limelight. We understand that if we esteem someone else more highly than ourselves (Philippians 2:3 KJV) we are not taking anything away from ourselves. Instead when we are able to do this, it shows just how strong or big we really are.

CHAPTER THREE

CLOSING THE GAP

(Relationships Need Support)

A gap is an opening or breach that allows passage from one area to another. Gaps are great when they are expected and there are times and specific areas in which gaps are necessary. When necessary, gaps can help for smooth operations or performance. However when gaps are not necessary or maybe not expected, there is the possibility for problems.

In these situations, gaps could create serious problems or maybe even prove to be detrimental. Because gaps are an opening, when weight or pressure is applied, the gap causes support to be diminished. Gaps could develop in our relationships and could cause problems. There are times that a person may need space in a relationship. However, for the most part, relationships need to be close and the people in them need to be supported for the relationship to develop and grow properly.

When a person, place, or thing is not properly supported sags or gaps could develop in the structure because something is missing. Support is such a vital element in relationships that without it, the relationship could begin to suffer. When something is missing anything could possibly try to fill the void. Unfortunately, many times the thing that tries to fill that void is not what is needed. Therefore the gap could remain and even grow.

Just as an unsupported structure that suddenly and unexpectedly has pressure applied is likely to collapse; the same is true for relationships. They may stand for a while without collapsing. However, if the pressure continues and support has not been given, the ultimate result may be a collapse or maybe even destruction to the relationship.

Over the years, we develop many different relationships.

We have relationships that are personal, professional, intimate, platonic, sexual, open, closed, and even estranged. These relationships are those we develop with people, places, and things.

Yes, we develop relationships with places and things as well as people. There are people, you may even know some of them, who develop such a relationship with a specific restaurant that they have a special place in the heart of the staff that comes and goes. Many times these people do not even have to look at a menu or be asked what they are ordering; the staff knows when to expect them and what they will be having.

We develop all kinds of relationships. Yours might not be to the extreme as the person who is known at the local restaurant. You may have one where, despite how long it has been since your children graduated and left their school, your presence is expected at every home sporting event the school hosts. We develop these relationships for many reasons. Some of them makes perfectly good since to those on the outside, while others may think they are completely foolish or even laughable. Whatever reason a person develops the relationship he or she develops, bottom line is; to them it makes perfectly good sense.

Some of the relationships we develop last for years, while others may be for a short while. Regardless to the types of relationship we may develop or be involved in, we have to put fort an effort to manage them. Some relationships require more managing than others, but the management is still needed. Even with appropriate management, there is the opportunity for gaps or breaches to develop. These gaps or breaches could pose serious problems.

So, what could cause a gap or breach? Difficulties in our relationships could cause gaps or breaches to form. These difficulties could develop as the result of one person in the relationship having some type of an issue with another person in the relationship.

However, it is also possible that even good situations in our lives could cause a gap or breach to form. Think about it, when something good or positive happens in our lives, we want to share those things with the people we know and care for. Sometimes, even these people, those we care for, may become upset (jealous) with the positive situation we are experiencing. Yes, it is possible for those we care for to become jealous and maybe even covetous of things we possess or may be happening in our lives. When or if this happens, gaps or breaches could form. Consider the story of Joseph, who was known for having and interpreting dreams (Genesis 37 KJV). Joseph became hated by his brothers because their father favored him. They also hated him because of the dream he shared with them. Joseph's brothers thought Joseph, who was younger, was telling them that they would bow to Joseph one day. The feelings of hatred Joseph's brothers had towards him caused gaps to form in their relationships. Because the gaps were not dealt with, they remained for years, and ultimately led to, what seemed to be the detriment of the relationship with the boys.

Just as a structure may not be able to stand when pressure is applied, it is important to remember that the same is true in our relationships. The pressure could cause a collapse which could lead to unrecoverable detriment of a relationship. The hatred Joseph's brothers had towards him caused them to do the unthinkable. Once they got started, it was difficult to undo what they did to their brother.

Joseph loved and cared for his family and it is likely that he never would have tried to rule over them. However, his brothers were so blinded by jealousy and hatred that they could not or would not consider any other possibilities other than what they thought. They devised an evil scheme to kill him. All of this because Joseph shared his dream with them. The gap that was between Joseph and his brothers was severe and it was there for years. The gap began because of the love Joseph's father had for him. Although Joseph was not the oldest or the youngest child, his father loved him more than all his brothers (Genesis 37:3), which caused animosity between Joseph's older brothers.

Joseph's father did not know how to show the love he felt without showing favoritism. Therefore he poorly communicated this love to his son in the presence of his children. Poor communication is a sure way to develop gaps or breaches in relationships.

So if poor communication is a strong force and possibility to developing gaps or breaches, could good communication close them? Yes, good communication is a way to close the gaps of misunderstandings and assumptions. Joseph's father could have communicated his love for Joseph in a better manner which could have prevented the hatred of his brothers. With good communication, one could encourage people by showing them support during difficult and even good times. Good communication could be vital to the success or health of a relationship. Good communication has the ability to generate and bolster positive outcomes; thus closing any gaps caused by inconsistencies or misconceptions.

The words that are used in good communication basically allow us to let those we are communing with know that they are not standing alone.

In essence, we are letting them know that we are there for them. We are ensuring them that we are with them and when times get hard, we will help them stand. Good communication also allows them to know that we are also there to laugh with them and share the good times with them as well. We give encouraging words to family, friends, co-workers, neighbors, and even strangers.

Just as physical structures need support beams in various locations and of various sizes, the support we provide through encouraging words and actions have various impacts. What seems like a simple word to one could be a life changing word for another. A smile may not seem like a big deal, but to someone struggling with depression or having a bad day for any reason, that smile could be uplifting. The impact of our encouraging words could vary from one person to another, but the fact remains; each of us need support at various times to help us to stand. The support we need will not always look the same. Sometimes we may need an encouraging word, while at other times we may need a more supportive action to help us stand. Sometimes we may be okay with support being given behind the scene. However, there may also be times that we need the support we receive to be more prevalent; meaning we need as many people as possible to know about the support we are receiving.

Regardless to the amount of support that is needed, the bottom line is, it is needed, in good and bad situations. Without it we may not be able to remain upright.

Standing alone could cause us to crumble under pressure. If pressure causes us to crumble, we may not be able to recover, which could ultimately be detrimental to our relationships. Think about it; if you are working on a job in which you do not have the support of those you are working with or for you may begin to feel unappreciated. When we feel unappreciated, regardless of the relationship, it is likely that you may not begin to look for another relationship. If those we love or care for never have anything positive, uplifting, or encouraging for us we may find ourselves rethinking that relationship. No one wants to be with someone who does not appreciate them. Or who never shows that they appreciate them.

That's what closing gaps is all about; showing the men, women, and children in our lives that we appreciate them.

There are so many obstacles that we face throughout our day to day activities, our direct relationships should not be one of them. Our personal relationships as well as those with organizations should be comforting and supportive, not disruptive or abusive.

So what do you do, if you find yourself in a relationship that is not comforting or supportive? Do you leave or get out of the relationship?

Remember this; all relationships require work.

One puts into a relationship what he or she wants to get out of the relationship. This is true with all of the relationships we develop throughout our life; relationships with the many people, places, and even things that we encounter. Most of the time, we conscientiously put forth a strong effort to ensure we are making them the best possible relationship they can be. However, there are times that not everyone in the relationship is as eager about working at making it great.

For most of, relationships could give us a sense of belonging or being. For the most part, all of us want to belong to something or be a part of something. So we work at developing relations that will help us to be a part of something that is bigger and better than who and what we are alone. After we develop our relationships, next we take the necessary steps to make them grow. Yes, we grow our relationships. Just as we grow naturally, our relationships should grow.

Think about it, if a child is not growing, we will begin seeking professional help to determine what the problem is and how we can solve it. We do this because we care for the child and we want to see him or her grow into strong successful adults. Well, if we care for our relationships, we must also seek care. If our relationships are not growing, we should begin communicating with those involved to see what the problem is and how we can solve it. We would never assume that a none-growing child is okay and will hit his or her growth spirt soon. Although not all relationships grow at the same rate, there should be some recognizable growth within the relationship. We also should not make this assumption with our relationships. Of those involved in the relationship, someone needs to care enough to identify any retardation and seek help.

We should want and should strive to make our relationships better every day. By this time next year, our relationships should look better, sound better, and be better than they are right now.

Just as our interests change over the years, as we grow older, so should our relationships.

So, how do we grow them? How do we make them better?

We grow our relationships in many ways. One of the ways we grow them is through encouragement (effective communication) and support. Together we stand, divided we fall. This phrase encourages unity and support. It suggests that there is strength when we join together. In most cases, two or more people will be able to do more than just one person, suggesting that there is strength in numbers. Think about it; if you are in an intimate relationship with someone, chances are you will marry that person. Therefore, your relationship just went from you and the person to you and their family and friends. Same is true for those non-intimate relationships. We develop a relationship with one and gain many more.

We should expect to see continued growth and changes within our relationships. This growth will help to establish solid, no gap, healthy relationships. Relationships that are strong and able to stand the many tests that **will** come up against them. Some of these tests will be expected. For instance, some of the challenges that come with blended families will be expected. With step children, certain obstacles are expected. The children could be reluctant to accept a relationship with his or her new stepparent.

When we know what to expect, we can somewhat prepare for it. However, that is not always the case. Sometimes we are caught completely off guard by test and these surprises could really take its toll on us. Other times, we are not even sure what the problem is. Therefore we don't know how to remedy the problem. How can we get rid of what we do not know exist?

Knowing what the gap is will allow the gap to be closed effectively. In other words, once we identify a problem or what is causing a gap in our relationships, we can then effectively begin to remove it. If we never identify it, it will remain and the gap could grow.

A gap could be as simple as a misspoken word. If it is not addressed or dealt with other problems could form.

It is possible for one person in a relationship to say or do something that does not seem important or insulting. However to others in the relationship what it could be disrespectful, hurtful, or maybe even degrading. So what one sees as nothing, to another could be disastrous.

Unfortunately, although a person is bothered by something, sometimes he or she may feel that it is best to not say anything. They could make this decision for many reasons. Unfortunately, the unknowing person could repeat what was said or done, causing more pain. This could cause a gap to form which could be detrimental to the relationship.

Because we are all different, we do not always see things the same. Even siblings growing up in the same home can perceive and accept things completely differently. It is also possible for a person to change his or her mind over time. Just because someone allowed or accepted something once does not mean that he or she will continue to do so.

> **Remember this: when I was a child, I spoke as a child... (I Corinthian 13:11 KJV)**

As we live and grow older, our thoughts and actions should change. Therefore, it's okay if something we used to allow, we no longer want to accept. Just use god communication and make it known.

It is possible for a person, who is close to us to not realize he or she is saying or doing something that is hurting us. So we have a responsibility to be open enough and care enough to make it known to them. If they care for us, they will not want to hurt us and will most likely welcome the change.

However, unfortunately, there are people, sometimes those we are close to, who actually seek to hurt others. These people may seek ways to cause gaps or even pain in our relationship. Of course these people do not make it known that this is their intention. Therefore, years may go by before this is realized.

However, if we learn that someone is seeking our hurt or pain, we owe it to ourselves to seek help. Face it, had we known these people had such impure thoughts and were capable of hurting us, we **never** would have entered into a relationship with them. Share your concerns, pay attention to the warnings, offer help to make even this relationship healthy. But, if they are not willing to change, don't feel bad about seeking to end the relationship. As a matter of fact, if you share with someone that something he or she is doing is hurting you and they are **NOT** willing to change, **RUN!** This behavior would suggest the dam has broken and the breach is beyond repair. This gap may not be mendable.

Relationships are just as different as the people who make them up. Some relationships are for a lifetime while others are for a much shorter period.

The same is true with organizations we may be affiliated with. When we are in a relationship with someone or something we don't care who knows. We will show our support in many ways. We will wear our support like a badge of honor. We will let the world know how we feel. We will openly share our passion.

It is encouraging to know that someone is passionate about us. Therefore, through encouragement and support will close gaps. For this reason, it is vital and necessary for us to let those that we are passionate about know it. Share it, shout it from the mountain tops, no matter how you do it, make it known. The more you share it, the more encouragement and support you bring to that relationship.

CHAPTER FOUR

IT DIDN'T FEEL GOOD

(Wilderness Experiences)

A wilderness is designed to be an uncomfortable place. There are little to no provisions available in the wilderness. In the wilderness, wildlife is free to roam. The wilderness is not designed nor is it expected to be inhabited by humans. However, millions of people visit or consider visiting the wilderness each year. These people find their time spent in the wilderness to be acceptable, and even rewarding. The wilderness offers opportunities for people to explore, hunt, and retreat. The wilderness has the potential to offer spectacular views in which many people use to seek solace. However, the wilderness is also considered by many to desolate and useless.

One of the definitions of a wilderness is a state of neglect, powerless, or disfavor.

In most cases, when people talk about being in the wilderness, they are not speaking about a literal place. Instead, he or she is speaking of a difficult time in their life, recognized by many as a "wilderness experience". They may be experiencing a time in which he or she feels like they are alone in a dark and cold place. They may also feel like the pressures of life are weighing so heavy that it is impossible for them to make it to the much needed provisions necessary to stay alive. Many people have died in the wilderness. Many were exposed to the elements, which overtook them.

Many of us may have many of times in which we are in the wilderness. During these times, we may feel like everything we are trying to accomplish is impossible. It may feel like nothing is working. Many times, during wilderness experiences we believe we are going to die. During these times, we feel as though there is no relief. We may feel rejected, abandoned, unloved, and even unwanted.

While in these wilderness experiences, most of the time, we may not able to talk to anyone about what we are dealing with. During these times, we do not feel good. We can see no hope. During these times, it is possible to not even receive a positive word or deed from another. The illusion of the wilderness could have us blind to hope and faith.

Pain has a way of making us want to give up. While in the wilderness experience, we may believe that the only way out is to end it all. These wilderness experiences could come in many forms. They may come from work, personal relationships, family relationships, spiritual relationships, relationships we have with strangers, our neighbors, etc. While in these wilderness experiences, we may not understand why we there. We may not be able to see how any of what we are going through could possibly help us.

However, we must realize these wilderness experiences are **NECESSARY**. We must realize that the thing we are dealing with is building us. It is making us strong. It is helping us to grow. Sometimes those tough situations help us to realize that we need to make some changes in our lives. Sometimes we realize that people who we are involved with may not be the best for us. They may not have our best interest in mind.

Many times it is when we are alone that we are able to focus on us. All the distractions that have allowed us to ignore our own personal growth are removed and we are forced to pay attention to ourselves.

Sometimes we can get so focused on trying to help others that we lose ourselves. Thankfully those wilderness experiences have a way of causing us to deal with us. Like I said, in the wilderness, there is not much human activity in the wilderness. Therefore, when we are there, there are not many people we can call on. Not many people are willing to come to an uncomfortable place to try to help us.

Therefore, the wilderness experiences are for our benefit. Romans 8:28, "for we know all things work together for good…" This means that, even those things that do not feel good to us are actually working for us. More specifically, they are working for our good. Psalms 34:19, "Many are the afflictions…" So even if it seems that there is one wilderness experience after another with little to no relief, we should still rejoice in knowing that unless we decide to give up, we will not end in the wilderness. We will come out of the wilderness as overcomers.

Think about this; if we are never challenged, many of us will remain comfortable and complacent. We will most likely never push ourselves to do more, to be more than we are right now. We would be satisfied with letting someone else handle all the heavy lifting.

Who would not welcome an opportunity to not have to struggle? Not many of us. Therefore, although it will not be easy all the time, try to focus on what things will be like when you make it through to the other side. Think about the most rewarding time you have ever had in your life. Focus on believing that when you come out of this wilderness experience, it will be much more rewarding than even that.

When we go through difficult situations we sometimes call trials and/or storms (wilderness experiences), we figure out ways to help others from going through what we have gone through. We try to make a difference for someone who may be coming up after us.

Even when you find yourself in a place where you have done some things that seems like you will not be able to recover. Remember, you will not end in the wilderness, unless you just decide to stay there. Sometimes we may deal with a situation for so long that it seems like we have been in a wilderness experience for years, but don't give up. When lost in the wilderness, it seems there really is no way out. All you can see for miles and miles is nothing. It seems, all hope is lost; still, don't give up.

I like to believe that as long as there is life, there is hope. Even if it seems like the life that remains is not healthy enough to go on, there is still hope. If you don't give up, God will not give up. And if God will not give up on you, why would you ever consider giving up on him.

Yes, sometimes it seems like, despite trusting God and expecting him to provide a way of escape or maybe even to keep us out of struggles in the first place, he has forgotten about us. Remember, as Jesus hung on the cross, he cried, what is translated to "why hast though forsaken me?" (Matthew 27:46 KJV). If Jesus, whose purpose for being born was to die for you and I, felt as though he was forsaken and left alone, we are not exempt. Meaning we cannot avoid feeling this way at least once in our lives. However, just as this was not the case for Jesus, this is not the case for you either. You are not alone and just like Jesus' life has been used to make a difference to the lives of millions you too have a purpose that is much greater than you can imagine.

Remember, in a wilderness there is not much human activity; only a few adventurers every now and then. Therefore the hopelessness you may be feeling may be stronger than you ever thought possible, but don't give up. There is a plan for you.

Wilderness experiences come into our lives for many reasons. Sometimes we are completely responsible for the wilderness we may find ourselves in. However, there are also times that we may be led in the wilderness by another. Jesus was led into the wilderness by the spirit (Matthew 4:1 KJV). It was necessary for him to go into the wilderness, so the spirit led him there. According to the scripture, he was led in the wilderness to be tempted. Jesus knew why he was being led in the wilderness and there may be times that we know why we are there. When we know, we are more likely to be able to stay there until the situation comes to an end because we know what we will get when we come out. We won't jump ship or run away in the midst of the storm. When we know, we understand that something is being worked out in us, through us, or for us. Or maybe all of these.

However, most of the time, we do not know why we are there. When we do not know why we are in the wilderness, it makes it that much harder to remain. One of the great things about not knowing is that all we have to do is ask. Growing up I was taught, "don't question God" but through the bible, we are told, "come, let us reason together..." (Isaiah 1:18 KJV). If we do not understand a thing, how will we ever, if we do not ask a question?

Keep this in mind; our perception is just that, "ours". We have a right to interpret and perceive things however we want. Are you a negative person, always finding the bad in something? Or are you a positive person who can find the good in anything? Are you a glass half empty or half full type of a person? In the midst of a storm, our attitude could be the sunshine someone, including ourselves, needs. Sure situations have the ability to make us feel a certain way, but remember; you control your attitude. Don't surrender your power to anyone or anything. When you allow the situation to cause you to act a certain way, that's what you are doing. If you are going to let it do anything, let it cause you to do good. What I mean by this is, if someone is making you angry, most likely that is what they are trying to do. So, don't give in. Instead, let your anger push you into making them angry by **NOT** giving them what they want. Proverbs 15:1 talks

Jennifer Webb Farris

about a kind word turning away wrath. Romans 12:20 talks about how being kind to your enemy will anger them much more than doing what they expect you to do.

While in the wilderness, someone is definitely watching and waiting to see how we will handle it. When we make it through we are able to help them. The strength we show, even if that strength is totally relying on the strength of God, gives them strength.

Life is a journey. We are constantly moving, traveling from one point to another. It is up to us whether we go forward, standstill, go backwards, or spend years going around in circles. Sure there are times that we will move forward quickly, while at other times it may seem as though there has not been any movement at all. It may seem as though, despite our best efforts, we are standing still with no movement at all. Standing still is not always a bad thing. Sometimes we need to stand still so we can pay attention and see what is really happening. Standing still can help us to see ourselves and focus on what we are or should be doing.

Keep this in mind; we cannot get from one point to another without traveling. Therefore we should have some type of movement. Sometimes, a do over or going backwards could be helpful. Although we should not make it a habit of going backwards, it is better for a person who is going the wrong way to backup instead of continuing to travel in the wrong direction.

We should not spend too much time trying to figure out why we are in a wilderness experience. Instead, we should focus on what we know. Remember, a wilderness is not cultivated nor is it designed for human habitation. Therefore, pitch a tent for the time that you have to be there, but do not build your house there. There is little comfort in the wilderness, therefore, go **through** your wilderness experiences. Keep it moving. Use the wilderness to hunt, explore, or even retreat (get away from it all), but don't stay there.

CHAPTER FIVE

IT'S NOT OVER

(It Was Necessary)

Life has a way of presenting many unexpected situations. Some consider these unexpected situations to be "life happening". These situations may range from good to fantastic or from bad to worst. These situations may catch us completely off guard or we may have somewhat of an expectation of them. Either way, when "life happens" for the most part, there will be some type of a change to follow the situation.

The unexpected situations or life happenings we experience may take us on various adventures and/or journeys. We may be on one adventure or journey at a time or we may experience multiple at the same time. An adventure is defined as "an undertaking usually involving danger and unknown risks." A journey is "something suggesting travel or passage from one place to another." The adventures or "life happening" we experience may not necessarily have danger associated with them. However, if we are not careful or mindful while dealing with or going through this situation, we may actually bring danger to ourselves. We will set or chose some of these adventures or journeys for ourselves; while others may be forced upon us. No matter how we get there, the bottom line is, we are there. The important thing then becomes, what are we going to do now that we are there?

As previously discussed, Joseph was betrayed by his brothers who did despicable things to him. Their initial thought was to kill Joseph. However, Joseph's destiny could not allow this, therefore, they changed their minds and ended up just selling him into slavery. Joseph nor his brothers knew what his or their destiny was and neither do we. We may have an ideal or may know where we want to be, but the road leading to our destiny is full of unexpectedness. Joseph nor his brothers grew up knowing that one day their lives would take the paths they found themselves on. This is that unexpectedness. We know that greatness is in us. We know we want to make an impact in the lives of others, but we don't really know how that greatness or impact will come about.

Joseph and his brothers suddenly found themselves on an adventure or journey that changed their lives forever. Joseph did not choose this path for himself. Although his brothers chose to do what they did, they did not know their lives would be affected as they were. They had to live with the situation they created. Joseph and his brothers did not realize that this path set Joseph in place to bring his dream to fruition. Therefore, this adventure or journey Joseph was forced into was necessary to get Joseph to bring him to his place of destiny. The place we find ourselves in, may be uncomfortable and maybe even frightening. There may be situations that cause us to think that our lives are actually in danger, but it could be that this place is necessary to bring up to our destiny. Why would Joseph or anyone else think it is a bad thing to share our dreams with those we are closest to?

For the most part, we don't. Joseph shared his dream with those he trusted, yet they were not able to receive what Joseph shared with them. Instead they were bothered and insulted by the thoughts that he would have such a dream.

These were people who were most familiar with Joseph. They knew his upbringing; it was the same as theirs. However, jealousy caused them to be blinded and it tainted their thinking. The zeal we feel when we have a dream sometimes may be indescribable, yet we take a shot at doing so. Sometimes we do more damage in trying to share it, or maybe we share it too soon. Yet it is also possible that sometimes, when a person is familiar with us and knows where we come from, it is difficult for them to receive or appreciate our dreams.

Jesus was not accepted by those who should have been closest to him. John 1:11 says that "he came unto his own and his own received him not." Sometimes the encouragement that we need or the push we need to go to the next level is not going to come from the people or person we expect it to come from. This does not mean that these people do not love or care for us. This could happen for many reasons.

Keep in mind that, although Joseph did not plan or chose the journey or adventure he found himself on, without this path, he would not have found himself in the place where his dream could come to pass.

Sure, we expect the people who love and care for us to be our greatest support. However, this may not always be the case. Sometimes, these people can be our greatest adversaries. However, whether we are supported or not, we must remember, "It is not over." The adventure or journey, whether favorable or not, is NOT the end and it may very well be what is necessary to bring us to our place of destiny. As long as we have breath we have more living to do. Sure living is full of unknown risks and passageways. Sometimes the adventure or journey may simply be, having to realize that those we love and care for do not support us.

For most of us, this is a struggle. We expect these people to have our back when everyone else walks away. However, for whatever reason that may not be the case. When someone we look to for encouragement, turns their back to us, especially if this person is family, we may be afraid to look for or expect encouragement from anyone else. We may think, if those closest to us do not accept us, why would someone who knows little to nothing about us. Remember, It is NOT Over, sometimes it is necessary to get us to a place of not relying on anyone. Sometimes we have too many people around us and we end up getting complacent not trying to push ourselves to greatness. Don't let this stop you. It may be painful and seem like we are all alone, but don't worry if we don't give up, we will soon realize It's Not Over!

Joseph and Jesus were completely rejected by those who should have supported them. However, their stories did not end there. Just as their stories did not end with the pain of rejection, neither will our story end there, if we keep moving. Sure the pain may be strong and may be even unbearable at times but remember, it is a passage way. There may be some unknown risks associated with rejection, but It's Not Over.

There is a plan for our rejection. That plan is to make us stronger. That plan is to cause us to go to a place where we can make a greater impact.

The rejection of Joseph and Jesus was good in that it allowed them to help more people. Remember, when God gives us a dream, when he has a plan, no one can stop it. Sometimes we may stand alone. There may even be times that we have to encourage ourselves to remember this, but whatever it takes, remember, It's Not Over". No matter how long it takes, continue to wait and expect the dream to come into fruition. Sometimes the wait is longer than others but remember, "It's Not Over."

There may be times that we have to make adjustments because of the changes in lives. These adventures or journeys may cause us to be in a land surrounded by strangers; just as it was with Joseph. We may even have to rely on these strangers to help us, just as it was with Joseph. He found more favor with Potiphar (Genesis 39) than with his own family. There may also be times when we think, just as Joseph did that we have made it to our place of destiny, only to have another adventure or journey to begin suddenly.

This was the case with Joseph. Suddenly and unexpectedly he found himself on another adventure or journey. Joseph did the right, however it seemed as though he was punished for doing so. Many times we may feel as though we are doing what is right only to have things unfold much differently than what we expected. Instead of being rewarded for the doing the right thing, Joseph was thrown in prison. We too may be doing all the right things, only to seem like nothing good is coming of it. We may not be physically thrown into a prison cell. However, this could cause us to be imprisoned in our minds. This imprisonment could be worse than an actual physical imprisonment. The mind is strong and could cause us to cause many other stressors to develop. Even in these, we must encourage and remind ourselves, not to give up, say the words, "It's Not Over."

It may seem like we are in a reprise, coming out of one struggle and right into another without any type of serenity. Rejections and struggles do not feel good. Rejection causes us to feel alone and unwanted. Many times the rejection will cause us to question our abilities and relationships. We will sometimes wonder, what is wrong with me? This may cause of the begin making changes to who we are. Changes are not always bad. However, they are not always needed. Joseph did not have to make any adjustments to his character or any of his behaviors. He simply needed to endure to the end of the many adventures and journeys he found himself on. Although Joseph had not seen his family in years, he never lost sight of the dream.

Regardless to how we feel, we cannot lose sight of our dream. Even if we are the only one believing our dream will come to pass, we must keep on believing. Sometimes it may seem like it is taking too long and things are getting too far off track, but we have to remind ourselves of the dream. Sometimes we may have to put an image of the dream somewhere we can see it regularly to help remind us and to keep us focused on it. "Write the Vision..." (Habakkuk 2:2 KJV) this allows us to keep the vision on our mind. Therefore, we will stay focused on why we are doing what we are doing. Staying focused will help us remember why we cannot give up. It will help us to realize that by overcoming the pain associated with rejection and struggle we will be able to help someone else. The rejection and struggles do not come to kill us, although many times, while dealing with them, it feels like we are dying. Instead of focusing on the rejection and struggle, we should keep our mind on the dream. Focus on the outcome we want to see. Focus on the end result, not the pieces.

When putting a puzzle together, we do not spend time looking at the individual piece. We get the image of the completed picture in our head and we work to make the pieces look like that. It is perfectly okay if we have to glance back at the picture to remember what it looks like. This may be why Habakkuk was instructed to "Write the Vision". Sometimes it may take so long for the fruition of the dream that we and maybe even those we shared our dream with, forget what the dream is to look like. That's okay, look back, look back several times if needed, but don't lose site of the dream.

We must remember, the adventure or journey may be long and unknown, but it is necessary for us to continue because the passageway wherewith we are traveling will take us to our place of destiny. After we make it to our place of destiny, we will be able to help bring about a change and maybe even save the life of even those who rejected and hurt us along the way. We have a choice. We could refuse to go through the struggles and pain, but where will that get us?

We must remind ourselves, sometimes over and over, that I will make a difference for someone other than myself if I continue and not give up.

Tell yourself, It's Not Over!

Wherever we are, regardless to what we are dealing with; if the dream has not come to pass and there is breath left in our body, it is not over. We may have to make some changes in how we thought the dream would look, but don't be discouraged. Joseph knew his brothers would one day bow to him, but he never expected it would be because he was second in command in the nation. Joseph's dream did not just make a difference for him and his family, but for his entire nation.

No matter where our dreams take us, we should try out best to enjoy the ride. We should also keep dreaming. Don't stop dreaming just because things were or are difficult. When one dream comes to fruition, dream again. As long as we are living we should find ourselves looking for the next big thing.

Remember this; regardless to what it looks like, It's Not Over. It is Necessary for us to overcome and continue, because we still have the opportunity to do and be more.

CHAPTER SIX

IT'S FOR MY GOOD

(He Knows Where You Are)

Whether we are in an unexpected place or a place where we purposed ourselves to be, God knows just where we are. As a matter of fact, he is with us. When things are good and descent, he is there with us. When things are difficult and tough, he is there with us. Isaiah 41:10 (KJV) says, "Fear not, I am with thee…" He reassures us, "he will never leave nor forsake us…" and "nothing can separate us from his love."

He knows that from the time we are born until we die, we develop ideals or thoughts about things that make us happy or things that feel good to us. He knows that these things may be healthy and helpful and keep us on the right path throughout life. He also knows that sometimes these things that keeps us sane or makes us happiest are things that may not necessarily be good for us. He does not give us the okay to indulge in these unhealthy or impure things. Instead he gives us a way of escape to get out of these things.

Some of the things we develop include habits in our lives that could cause problems for us and/or those we love and care for. He knows that when we develop these habits we will most likely try to keep others from knowing about them. We try to hide these things because we are ashamed that we. He knows that most of the time we try to hide these things because we do not want our family to know about them. We don't want them to worry and we also don't want to receive the scolding we may receive by them knowing about these things that are not good to or for us.

There are many habits we develop over the years, we need to understand that he knows about each of these habits, whether they are good or bad. Everything that is done in darkness come to the light therefore, there is no need in hiding it. By hiding it, we are only prolonging the inevitable. Our family members and/or those we care for will eventually find out about these things.

When we realize that he knows exactly where we are and what we are dealing with, there is no need in trying to conceal a thing. When we try to conceal a thing we will most likely lie to keep it concealed. Lying only creates other problems. There is nothing that can be hidden from him. Even when we do not let anyone know what we are dealing with, he knows.

The Lord may allow a secret fault to continue for years. This does not mean that the Lord is not able to fix the problem. It also does not mean that he accepts or wants us to remain in the thing. He allows them for many reasons. It could be that he allows the thing to continue for personal growth of ourselves or for that of a loved one. Even secret faults could be used to help us. In Psalms 19:12 David asks God to cleanse him from secret faults. Problems and secret faults do not discriminate, anyone can be affected by them. David was the king, yet he found himself trying to conceal some of the things he did.

Even if we find ourselves in a difficult situation because of something we actually did that was not right, he is with us. Sure there may be some type of consequence that we have to deal with, but we can rest assured that he is with us. Not only is he with us, if we let him, he will fight for us. When we come to ourselves and realize that we he has us in his hand. Job said, "In his hand is the soul (life) of every living thing... (Job 12:10 KJV). We are his children and he is our father and he wants to take care of us. He wants to work it out for us.

If we trust him, we will find ourselves understanding what Paul wrote in Romans 8:28. No matter how things look, feel, or sound, if we love God, it is working for our good. That bad situation, although it seems to be the worst thing that could ever happen to us, is actually working for us. It may take a little while, or it may take long while but if we don't give in and if we keep moving forward, we will realize, it is going work out so that we benefit from it.

It may seem like there is no hope and there is nothing we can do to make the situation better, but if we hold out and keep moving forward, we will soon see just how it is working for our good.

There is a plan for that situation that we are suddenly or maybe unexpectedly finding ourselves dealing with. The plan may be one that we never even considered prior to entering into the situation. We may have had our plan drawn and placed in a perfect binder to remind us of what the plan is, only to have a new plan suddenly come to us. Think about it, how many people have suddenly had to make adjustments to their walk of life due to the unexpected birth of death of a loved one.

Many young people have set their plan for after high school only to have these plans altered by an unexpected pregnancy. Many were offered scholarships or acceptance into college only to have these plans changed due to the unplanned pregnancy. Sometimes these people struggled and were not able to get back to their dream. However, many times, the birth of a child gave the parents a drive they never had and they were able to apply themselves in ways they never even imagined.

Difficult and unexpected situations have a way of causing us to want to get beyond the difficulty. Most of us are not comfortable with unexpectedness, therefore, we will diligently work to get back to a place of certainty. This is done best when we are positive and eager to not give in. Positivity has a way of encouraging us. Difficult situations have of way of being a driving force to push us to our place in destiny, even when we do not know what our destiny is.

Sometimes we may not be pushing ourselves far or hard enough. Sometimes we may have gotten comfortable staying on the shore, when we really should be launching out to the deep. Many times we have gotten comfortable sitting in the boat, when we really need to get out of the boat and go along shore. Lots of time we get comfortable and do not want to change. However, difficulties and unexpectedness causes us to sometimes go to those places we did not want to on our own.

Many times we drag the difficult situation out much longer than it was ever expected to be. When we focus on the problem and not on working towards finding a solution, we end up staying there too long. The children of Israel wandered in the wilderness for 40 years (Exodus 13 KJV). They should have only been there several days. It seemed as though they were just walking around, but through retrospect we understand that God was working some things out of them.

This is how it **works for our good.**

Many times there are things in us that we don't even know are there. The

The difficult situation is an opportunity for us to grow. It is a chance for us to make some changes. Many times we don't even know we need to make changes in our lives. Difficult times have a way of bringing out a person's true colors. It could be a personality adjustment that is needed. Or it could be something more serious, like a health concern.

There have been times that people never knew something was going on in their body until having some type of an accident. The health issue could have progressed in their body undetected for years. However, due to the need to see a doctor for issues surrounding an accident, the health issue was detected and could be treated. Undetected health concerns could cause many more problems or maybe even be detrimental if they remain undetected.

Therefore, it was good to have been involved in the accident. Sure, initially the accident could have seemed difficult and maybe even unfair. However, after learning about the health issue the accident may soon be forgotten. In other words, the accident worked for the good.

No matter where we are or why we ended up there, we should remember that the situation will work for our good, if we let it. Even when there is no good thing in the situation, there is a silver lining somewhere. Sometimes we have to work at finding it, but it is there. The Best is Yet To Come, therefore, keep moving. No matter where we are or who is with us, Never Give Up. Our Best Days Are Before Us, not behind Us (Haggai 2:9).

Forgive yourself for your faults
and your mistakes and move on.

Les Brown

Printed in the United States
By Bookmasters